AF426705

Table of Contents

"If you write a half hour a day it makes a lot of writing year by year."

— Gertrude Stein

WHY 100?

This little book is about the power of building a 100-word writing habit.

You may ask yourself, "Why would anyone bother building a 100-word writing habit? That's too little to make a difference!" That's why a 100-word habit is perfect.

100 words a day is enough to get you started. It's enough to build skills, so you can easily write much more than 100 words. It's enough to shatter myths that have held you back from writing. Moreover, 100 words per day adds up to much more than you expect. In the eight years it took James Joyce to write *Ulysses* he averaged less than 100 words a day!

On May 31, 2004, I wrote and published my first blog post. It's so bad, I won't bother sharing it here (if you search the web, you'll find it). Aside from what I had been assigned in school, or for my first "real" job, I had hardly written anything — and it showed in this blog post. There was no point to it. It's a paragraph that rambles on, with sentences that aren't well-structured. It even — spell-check be damned — has a misspelling.

"Do the best you can until you know better. Then when you know better, do better."

—Maya Angelou

But my first blog post got me started. Through writing and publishing my words, I got a job in Silicon Valley, then high-paying clients, then my first book deal. Today, I've written three best-selling full-length books, and many shorter books. I've spoken on four continents, and my books are translated into seven languages. Thousands of people subscribe to my newsletter or listen to my podcast, and I've sold more than 70,000 books. I'm a full-time writer, and spend my days reading about whatever interests me, and sharing what I've learned along the way.

> Clear writing is only possible with clear thinking, and clear thinking is only possible with clear writing.

The benefits I've reaped from building a writing habit don't stop with my professional life. I used to be mystified by people who could write well, and wondered why I couldn't do the same. *What's their secret?*, I wondered. Now I know, there is no secret. Clear writing is only possible with clear thinking, and clear thinking is only possible with clear writing.

Not every word I write is clear, but my writing habit has vastly improved my thinking and emotional resilience. This has made me more self-aware, arming me with the mental tools to handle nearly whatever challenge life throws my way. When I've gone through a bad breakup, been displaced from my home, tragically lost someone close to me, or had my life scrambled by a global pandemic, writing has been there to help me through it.

"The object of writing is to write to yourself, to let your self know what you have been trying to avoid."

—Bessel van der Kolk

When I wrote that first blog post, I was trapped in a toxic relationship, living in a town wanted out of, working a job I wanted to quit. With the help of writing, I've reinvented myself many times over. I've redesigned my life, informed by the introspection writing affords, and now live happily in South America, with a wonderful life partner.

That first blog post I wrote was little more than 100 words. I wish I could tell you I wrote 100 words the following day, and the day after that. Unfortunately, I had a lot of false beliefs about what, when, and how someone should write, so it was many years before I finally built a writing habit.

I mourn the loss of those years, and wonder what I could have accomplished if I had built a writing habit sooner. Hopefully, with the help of this book, you'll see the incredible power of a tiny writing habit, and won't make the mistake I did.

"[My paintings are] the pages of my journal…. The future will choose the pages it prefers. It's not up to me to make the choice."

—Pablo Picasso

A 100-WORD HABIT IS TOO SMALL TO FAIL

Before you picked up this book, how many words did you think was a good daily writing goal? Be honest! Most people think, a few thousand words. If they're being modest, maybe they shoot for one-thousand, or even five-hundred. Intuitively, 100 doesn't seem like enough.

But here's what happens when you try to write a thousand words a day: You do it the first day. Maybe you do it the second day. Maybe you do it for several days, or if you're really disciplined, a couple weeks. Inevitably, you miss a day. Maybe you get insanely busy. Or, maybe you sit down to write one day, and just can't.

"Every avalanche begins with the movement of a single snowflake, and my hope is to move a snowflake."

—Thomas Frey

What happens when you try to pick up the habit again the following day? That thousand-word goal looms large. You feel bad about missing a day and you're a little out-of-practice because you've missed a day, or more. Writing that first word seems hard enough as it is, but it's even harder, because you have that thousand-word goal. If one word seems hard, a thousand seems impossible. So you miss that day, the next, then completely forget you've ever aspired to have a writing habit at all.

> A GOOD HABIT STARTS WITH
> A GOAL TOO SMALL TO FAIL.

Most people think 100 words a day is too small a goal to even bother. And that's why it's the perfect goal: It's too small to fail. Even when you have a busy day, you can usually find the time and energy to write 100 words. And if you still miss a day, it's easy to get back into the habit.

TODAY IS THE BEST DAY TO START YOUR WRITING HABIT

An avalanche begins with a single snowflake. That's why I say that even though my first blog post was 100 words of pointless nonsense, it's the best post I've ever written: because it was responsible for so many changes in my career and life. Once you make the decision to write something, that single act leads to many more things.

This is why today is always the best day to start your writing habit. The sooner you get started, the sooner that simple action will lead to other things you can't foresee in this moment.

If you start a daily 100-word habit today, by one year from now, you will have written more than 36,000 words — that's the length of a novella, such as Stephen King's *Rita Hayworth and the Shawshank Redemption*, which got made into one of the greatest movies of all time, *The*

Shawshank Redemption. Or, that's enough to publish a seven-hundred-word blog post every week. At the rate of one novella or fifty-two blog posts a year, you could be incredibly prolific!

As you can see, a 100-word habit adds up to much more than you expect. But, as I'll show you next, the value of a 100-word habit is much more than the sum of its parts.

HOW TO WRITE A BOOK
100 WORDS AT A TIME

100 words
(one day)

700 words
(one week)

9000 words
(ninety days)

36,500 words
(one year)

HIDDEN COMPLEXITY TURNS SMALL ACTIONS INTO BIG RESULTS

Here's a brain teaser: How many people would have to be in a room for there to be a fifty-percent chance two of them have the same birthday?

Most people guess a hundred eighty, or at lowest a hundred. The actual answer?: twenty-three. If you have twenty-three people in a room, there's about a fifty-percent chance two of those people will have the same birthday.

How is that possible? With three-hundred sixty-five days in a year, intuitively, it seems amongst twenty-three people, there'd be about a one-in-fifteen chance of a shared birthday. We're talking about a one-in-*two* chance.

Scientists call this "the birthday paradox." It's a paradox because it's so counterintuitive. You don't have to understand how the math works out, but being aware of how our brains struggle to see this hidden complexity can help you see how small actions lead to big results.

HOW MANY PEOPLE UNTIL A 50% CHANCE OF A SHARED BIRTHDAY?

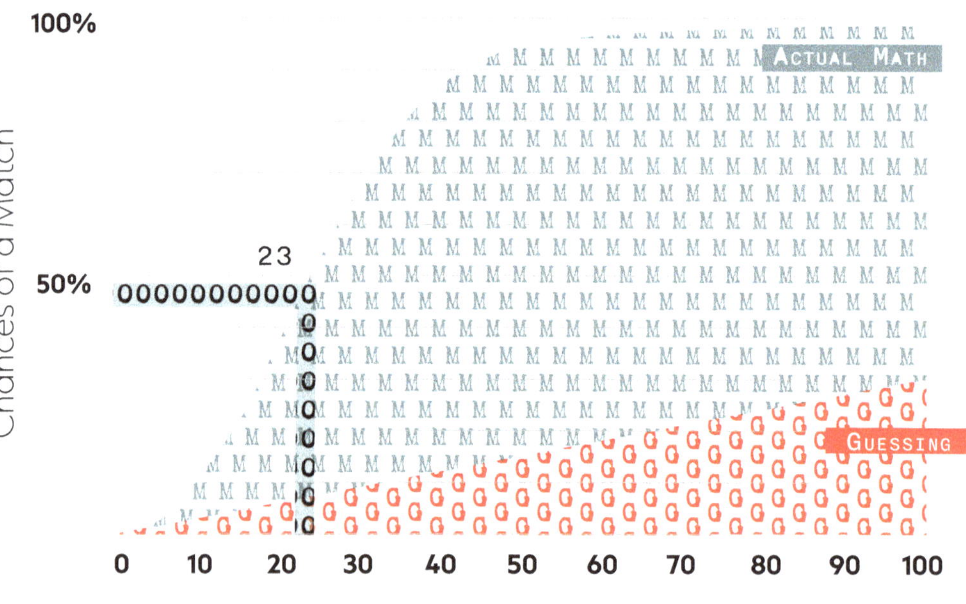

THE MAGIC OF COMPOUND INTEREST

What's equally counterintuitive is the power of compound interest. If you invested twenty dollars a month for forty years, at ten percent annual interest, how much money would you have at the end?

If you do the rough math in your head, it doesn't sound like much:

You're putting away two-hundred-forty dollars a year, for forty years, so that's nearly ten-thousand dollars.

Then you gain ten percent interest each year. Even if you had all ten-thousand dollars from the beginning, and earned a thousand dollars a year on interest, that'd be another forty-thousand, over forty years.

So, you might guess: You'd have about fifty thousand dollars saved up after forty years. Not that exciting.

The actual amount you'd have saving twenty dollars a month, gaining ten-percent interest each year, for forty years?: More than one-hundred thousand dollars. *Twice* our intuitive rough math.

COMPOUND INTEREST

INVESTING $20 A MONTH AT 10% YEARLY INTEREST

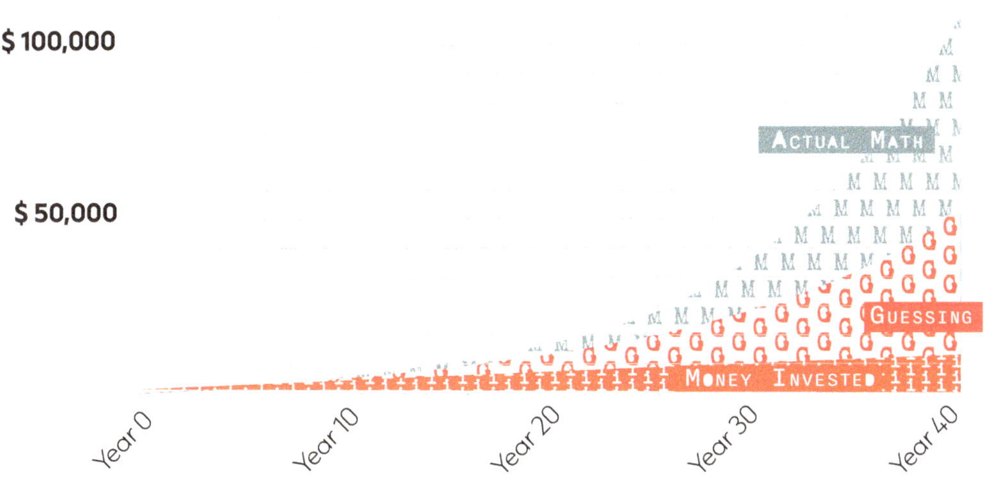

Both the birthday paradox and compound interest are counterintuitive, because we don't naturally think about how things interconnect. With each person we add to a room, we aren't just adding one potential birthday match. We're adding a potential match for each person already in the room. With each time we earn interest in an account, we aren't just earning interest on what we've invested. We're also earning interest on what we've gained all the previous times we've earned interest.

The same applies to a 100-word habit. It's a simple habit, and it's such a small number of words, it doesn't seem useful. But each day you write 100 words, you don't just add that 100 words to your lifetime output. Writing 100 words compounds upon all the other times you've written 100 words. You approach each day of writing with the collective experience of all the other days you've written.

> EACH TIME YOU WRITE, THE FORCE OF YOUR EFFORT IS MULTIPLIED BY ALL THE PREVIOUS TIMES YOU'VE WRITTEN.

There's a story I love about Picasso: He's sitting in a cafe, and a woman recognizes him. Understandably excited, she asks if he'll sketch something for her on a napkin, saying she'll gladly pay him for it. He scribbles something, hands her the napkin, and says, "That will be $10,000."

"$10,000!?," she exclaims. "But that only took twenty seconds."

"To draw this took twenty seconds," Picasso says. "But to learn to draw this in twenty seconds took twenty years."

I don't know if this actually happened. I've heard the story several times, and the price and time taken to draw has differed. But it illustrates the point that skills compound. Each time you write, the force of your effort is multiplied by all the previous times you've written.

If you write 100 words a day, you could complete a novella every year. But the longer you keep writing 100 words a day, the better those words turn out. So, a 100-word habit is more than just adding 100 words per day.

Growing, slow, then fast

You may have tried to build a writing habit before, but gotten frustrated when you didn't notice a drastic improvement in your writing. That's because growth is slow, then fast.

This is what makes it challenging to invest money. At first, you don't notice any benefits. But as you saw in the graph of compound interest, at some point the rate of growth increases rapidly.

Have you ever walked by a construction site where seemingly nothing was going on, for weeks on end? Then one day, there's suddenly a twelve-story building frame there. They were working on the foundation, but once they had that in place, it was easy to make progress. Building a writing habit can be like that. You might feel as if nothing is going on for a long time, then one day everything clicks, and your skill level skyrockets.

A WRITING HABIT IS LIKE A BUILDING FOUNDATION. YOU MAKE SEEMINGLY NO PROGRESS, THEN SUDDENLY YOUR SKILL TOWERS.

FIVE WRITING MYTHS

I didn't start writing until I was well into my adulthood. I realize now that I believed a lot of myths about writing. There are five of them:

1. YOU CAN WRITE, OR CAN'T
2. ONLY WRITE WHEN INSPIRED
3. USE EVERY WORD YOU WRITE
4. EVERY WORD HAS TO BE GOOD
5. WRITE FROM BEGINNING TO END

A little more about each of these myths.

WRITING MYTH 1:
You can write, or can't

The myth to end all writing myths is the belief that you can write, or you can't. In other words, people believe you either have a talent for writing, or you don't.

"I am always doing what I can't do yet in order to learn how to do it."

—Vincent van Gogh

Growing up, I personally hated to write. I figured I didn't have any talent as a writer, and nobody challenged that belief. It was a very "fixed-mindset" upbringing. Psychologist Carol Dweck has shown that if you have a fixed mindset — meaning you think your abilities are fixed, that will turn out to be true. You have to have a growth mindset, meaning you believe you can grow.

I dreaded my college English composition class. The first day, my professor said, "Write a paper on the Vietnam War." I dropped the class immediately.

"Whether you believe you can do a thing or not, you are right."

—Henry Ford

I needed English composition credits to get my degree, so I took it again at a college in my hometown, over the summer. That professor said, "Write a paper about your best friend." I got an A in the class. When the transcript arrived in the mail, my dad said, "No way you're my son!" (He was joking — but not. See what I mean? Fixed mind-set: If I had his genes, no way I could get an A in English composition.)

I knew nothing about the Vietnam War. I knew a lot about my best friend. Once I was writing about something I knew, suddenly writing was easy! Sometimes all you need is to approach a skill from the right angle.

WRITING MYTH 2:
ONLY WRITE WHEN INSPIRED

I resisted building a writing habit because I thought I should only write when I felt inspired. I didn't feel inspired every day, so why write every day? Sometimes I did feel inspired: I'd leap to my keyboard, and bang out an article. Then months would pass before I'd write again.

> SOMETIMES YOU'LL FEEL GREAT AND WRITE TERRIBLE. OTHER TIMES, YOU'LL FEEL TERRIBLE AND WRITE GREAT.

Don't get me wrong, inspiration is wonderful. I love it when my fingers dance effortlessly on the keys, and my thoughts appear on the page, as if I were transcribing perfectly-edited prose. But, unless you experience a freakish abundance of inspiration, to build a writing habit, you have to write even when you don't feel like it.

One reason to write even when you're not inspired is, you're probably not as good a judge as you think of how a writing session will go: Sometimes you'll feel great and write terrible. Other times, you'll feel terrible and write great.

Another reason to write even when you're not inspired is even when you think a writing session is or isn't going well, you often later find out you were wrong. Sometimes you think a writing session went great, but when you review the writing, you're bored to death. Other times, you suffer through writing, but when you review it, you're enthralled. Stephen King said, of writing his first hit novel, *Carrie*, "Sometimes you're doing good work when it feels like all you're managing is to shovel shit from a sitting position."

"Sometimes you're doing good work when it feels like all you're managing is to shovel shit from a sitting position."

—Stephen King

Furthermore, even when you think your writing is bad, it's often good (and, unfortunately, vice versa). Personally, some writing I've shared that feels obvious or uninteresting to me has resonated with readers in ways I never expected. Think of Picasso's approach to art: He said he treated paintings as "the pages of my journal.... The future will choose the pages it prefers. It's not up to me to make the choice."

And even when you start a writing session without feeling inspired, you never know what you'll discover. Sometimes you'll be laboriously chipping away, one word at a time, only to suddenly strike a vein. Words start flowing out of you, and you zoom past your word-count goal.

"Inspiration is for amateurs. The rest of us just show up and get to work."

—Chuck Close

But the most important reason to write even when you don't feel inspired is, it keeps you in practice. Even if writing today feels uncomfortable and forced — even if the writing turns out that way, too — that you wrote today makes tomorrow's writing better.

Like the great painter Chuck Close said, "Inspiration is for amateurs. The rest of us just show up and get to work."

WRITING MYTH 3:
USE EVERY WORD YOU WRITE

If you write 100 words a day, at the end of each year you could have a novella. It might turn out that way, but it definitely doesn't have to and probably won't.

You don't have to use every word you write. Lots of your writing will be re-wording ideas you've already written about, or writing thoughts that don't belong in a final piece, such as *[okay, this is the part where I insert an example]*. Even more of what you write will merely be a first draft, much of which you'll later re-write.

"I'm never sure what I think
until I see what I write."

—Carol Loomis

What does it mean to "use" the words you write, anyway? If you write in a journal — improving your thinking and processing your emotions — but nobody else reads it, did you "use" your writing? I say you certainly have. Treat your words like the "journal pages" that were Picasso's paintings. You don't always have to have a final product. Sometimes the process itself is useful.

If you expect to use every word you write, you put yourself under too much pressure to make them good — which brings us to the next writing myth.

WRITING MYTH 4:

EVERY WORD HAS TO BE GOOD

Every word you write does not have to be good. Much of what you write will be bad. That will always be the case, no matter how long you write, or how great a writer you become.

"By being willing to be a bad artist, you have a chance to be an artist, and perhaps, over time, a very good one."

—Julia Cameron

Perfectionism is a creativity catch-22: If you expect to be perfect, you can't take action. If you can't take action, you can't become bad, then eventually good — much less perfect.

If your writing isn't embarrassingly bad on a regular basis, you're doing yourself a disservice. You're missing out on ideas that seem bad, but are actually good. Give yourself permission to suck. You don't stand a chance to write well without first writing poorly.

> Give yourself permission to suck. You don't stand a chance to write well without first writing poorly.

As Julia Cameron said, "By being willing to be a bad artist, you have a chance to be an artist, and perhaps, over time, a very good one."

WRITING MYTH 5:
WRITE FROM BEGINNING TO END

I said earlier that I wasn't interested in writing as a kid. Well, there was one time: I decided I wanted to write a book, so I had my mom take out her typewriter. I wrote, "Once upon a time." Then I couldn't think of what to write next, so I quit. I didn't write voluntarily again for more than a decade.

One word after another: That's how books are read, not written. Start with whatever part comes easiest. That could be because it's what you know, it came in a strike of inspiration, or it's just easier. Worry later about where it belongs in the final product.

"The first draft of anything is shit."

—Ernest Hemingway

Expecting to write one word after another, from beginning to end, is a form of perfectionism and personal torture. Writing is hard enough as it is, without putting unnecessary restrictions on yourself.

THE THREE CS OF WRITING

Building a writing habit will be much easier if you focus on one skill at a time. Too often, we try to carry out our vision of perfection, and get frustrated when we're unable to achieve it.

There are three Cs to writing.

1. **Consistency**
2. **Courage**
3. **Craft**

Focus on one C at a time, and you'll build a writing habit that lasts.

Consistency

The first C of writing is Consistency: Can you consistently show up every day and write? As you build consistency, don't worry about publishing your words, or even making them good. Worry only about writing 100 words each day. They can be good, or bad. They can be for a project you're working on, or you can simply write what's on your mind.

New habits are fragile. If you worry about anything other than consistently writing 100 words each day, you run the risk of getting frustrated, and dropping the habit. Work only on writing consistently before you work on anything else.

"Be regular and orderly in your life, so that you may be violent and original in your work."

—Gustav Flaubert

Courage

The second C of writing is Courage: Do you have the courage to publish your writing? Only after you're writing consistently should you care whether you're publishing your work or not. If you sit down the first day of your 100-word habit determined not only to write those 100 words, but to also publish them, you run the risk of putting too much pressure on yourself.

Publishing your writing is an accomplishment in itself. It can be scary to put your work out there, knowing it could be better, worrying you said something wrong, or that someone will criticize it. There's nothing that can make that fear go away, but if you're going to publish your work regularly, you need to learn to relish that fear.

You might be more comfortable publishing your work for the first time under a different name. You'll be surprised how little reaction it gets. You might invent in your mind a thousand ways people will criticize it, but more likely, nobody will notice at all!

Craft

The third C of writing is Craft: Can you write well? When most people try to start a writing habit, they skip ahead and try to make sure all their writing is good. But you can't write well if you're not writing at all.

It's an especially good idea to put off worrying about craft until later, because this is the C with the longest lifespan. Yes, even if you become a professional writer, you'll struggle to be consistent or to have the courage to publish. But, there's no end to how much time and energy you could put into craft. There's no one best way to write, and you could try to excel at many different ways, if you wanted.

> You can't write well if you're not writing at all.

If you worry about building consistency, then courage, you'll be shocked how your craft improves anyway. Through the mere act of writing every day, you'll see improvements. It may seem as if you aren't improving at all, then *boom*, one day your writing will be great. Then, you'll have some off days, but if you keep it up, the good ones will keep coming, and increase in frequency.

WHY EVERY DAY?

The most powerful thing about a 100 word writing habit is writing every day. When I say, "every day," that could be literally every day, or some other schedule you choose, such as every weekday.

Whatever schedule you choose, don't take off more than two days in a row. The more frequently you write, the easier it will be. The longer it's been since you last wrote, the harder.

> **The more frequently you write, the easier it will be.**

There's a concept in neuroscience called "neuroplasticity." Your brain is "plastic": It's always changing based upon the thoughts you have and activities you perform. As the saying goes, "Neurons that fire together wire together." Just as footprints in the sand will slowly disappear the more times waves wash over them, your writing skills will slowly disappear the more days you pass without writing.

NEVER FAIL AGAIN

Every once in a while, you'll miss a day you didn't intend to. This might feel like a failure, but it's not. While you're aiming to write 100 words a day, don't get too caught up on the streak. Streaks are overrated. It's impressive if you're able to write 100 words a day for, say, 100 days, but what then happens when you inevitably miss a day? You say to yourself, "Now I have to start all over again. It will be another 100 days before I'm back where I was." And that makes it harder to begin again.

I once had a good streak of meditating every day, but deliberately broke it. I wanted to string together a good number of days, just to see how neuroplasticity would change my brain. But after eighty-nine days, I missed a day on purpose. Why? Because I knew if I got attached to my streak, I'd be less likely to keep meditating once I broke it. Quitting right before the milestone of ninety days reminded myself that the benefits of meditation are not about having a long streak.

Be patient with yourself. If you miss a day, treat yourself with the forgiveness you would a child who "ran away from home," only to come back two hours later, suitcase in hand and head hung low. Keep the door always open for your habit.

But, if you keep missing days, ask yourself why? The following tips will help you perform your habit more consistently:

- **Do your habit at the same time, in the same place, with the same tool, every day.** In a perfect world, you can do your habit at the same time, in the same place, with the same tool, every day. For example, 7:30 a.m., on your kitchen table, with your laptop and a cup of coffee. That way, the actions get ingrained in your mind, and you hardly have to think about it. Of course, the same time and place aren't always possible, but can you use the same tool? I do my 100-word habit with an AlphaSmart, which is a cheap, portable word processor, with no internet connection. Nothing can get in the way of my habit, and I even bring it when I travel.

- **Stack your habit with another habit.** Are there other things do you every day? Probably waking up, brushing your teeth, eating breakfast, and many other things. If you do your writing habit with one or two of these other things, you'll improve your odds of success. Stanford professor BJ Fogg calls this "habit stacking." For example, you might write just after waking up, and just before eating breakfast.

- **Write what comes easily.** If you struggle to keep up the habit, ask yourself if you're writing what comes easily. Let yourself write about whatever you want. You could even write 100 words about your struggle to keep writing every day.

- **Go back to the first "C."** Don't forget the three Cs of writing: Consistency, Courage, and Craft. If you keep missing days, maybe you're thinking too much about publishing your writing, or improving it. Forget the last two Cs, and focus only on Consistency.

"You must have a room, or a certain hour or so a day, where you don't know what was in the newspapers that morning, you don't know who your friends are, you don't know what you owe anybody, you don't know what anybody owes to you."

—Joseph Campbell

START YOUR HABIT TODAY

I hope this short book has given you the kickstart you need to start your 100-word habit. Remember, there's no better day to start than today. Just imagine what you will have accomplished a year from now.

A FREE EMAIL COURSE TO BUILD YOUR 100-WORD HABIT!

If you'd like some help starting your 100-word habit, I have a free 21-day email course.

Sign up at **http://100wordwritinghabit.com**

ABOUT THE AUTHOR

David Kadavy is a bestselling author whose books help people be productive when creativity matters. His books include *Mind Management, Not Time Management,* and *The Heart to Start.* He writes at least 100 words a day, on his 1953 Smith-Corona Super typewriter, or his AlphaSmart. He lives in a cabin in the mountains outside of Medellín, Colombia. Follow him on Twitter or Instagram at @kadavy.